NEW VANGUARD • 143

US CRUISERS 1883-1904

The birth of the steel navy

LAWRENCE BURR ILLUSTRATED BY IAN PALMER & JOHN WHITE

First published in Great Britain in 2008 by Osprey Publishing
Midland House, West Way, Botley, Oxford OX2 0PH, UK
443 Park Avenue South, New York, NY 10016, USA
E-mail: info@ospreypublishing.com

A CIP catalog record for this book is available from the British Library

ISBN: 978 1 84603 267 7

Page layout by Melissa Orrom Swan, Oxford
Index by Glyn Sutcliffe
Typeset in Sabon and Myriad Pro
Originated by PPS Grasmeme Ltd., Leeds
Printed in China through Worldprint Ltd.

08 09 10 11 12   10 9 8 7 6 5 4 3 2 1

For a catalog of all books published by Osprey Military and Aviation
please contact:

NORTH AMERICA

Osprey Direct, c/o Random House Distribution Center, 400 Hahn Road,
Westminster, MD 21157

E-mail: info@ospreydirect.com

ALL OTHER REGIONS

Osprey Direct UK, P.O. Box 140 Wellingborough, Northants, NN8 2FA, UK

E-mail: info@ospreydirect.co.uk

Osprey Publishing is supporting the Woodland Trust, the UK's leading
woodland conservation charity, by funding the dedication of trees.

www.ospreypublishing.com

ARTISTS' NOTE

Readers may care to note that the original paintings from which the
color plates in this book were prepared are available for private sale.
All reproduction copyright whatsoever is retained by the Publishers.
All inquiries should be addressed to:

John White (artist for plates D and E)
5107 C Monroe Road
Charlotte
NC 28205
USA

The Publishers regret that they can enter into no correspondence upon
this matter.

AUTHOR'S ACKNOWLEDGMENTS

The author wishes to acknowledge the help and assistance of the following:
Megan Fraser, Library Director; Craig Bruns, Curator; Jesse Lebovics,
Manager Olympia/Becuna, and Matt Herbison, Curatorial Associate,
Independence Seaport Museum; John Hattendorf; Ernest J. King, Professor
of Maritime History, Naval War College; Mark Hayes, Naval Historical Center;
Chris Havern, US Coast Guard Historical Office; Stephen Davies, Hong Kong
Maritime Museum; Jenny Wraight and Iain MacKenzie, Royal Navy Historical
Branch; Dr Nicholas Lambert; and my wonderful wife, Judi, who first
introduced me to the USS Olympia and the Theodore Roosevelt Museum
at Sagamore Hill.

AUTHOR'S DEDICATION

To my grandfather, John Fletcher, a professional soldier in the British Army,
who served throughout World War I, including service in Murmansk
alongside crew members of the USS Olympia.

EDITOR'S NOTE

For ease of comparison between types, imperial measurements are used
almost exclusively throughout this book. The following data will help in
converting the imperial measurements to metric:

1 mile = 1.6km
1lb = 0.45kg
1 yard = 0.9m
1ft = 0.3m
1in. = 2.54cm/25.4mm
1 gal = 4.5 liters
1 ton (US) = 0.9 tonnes

Please note that all uncredited images are courtesy of the US Naval Historical Center.

INDEPENDENCE SEAPORT MUSEUM

Independence Seaport Museum on the Delaware River showcases the
region's maritime heritage, with: two floors of exhibition galleries; a
working wooden boat shop; the National Historic Landmark 1892 Cruiser
Olympia and the World War II Submarine Becuna; a concert hall; children's
educational programs and adult tour programs; special events; a research
archive and library; and a gift shop.

211 S. Columbus Blvd. & Walnut St.
Philadelphia

Tel. (001) 215-413-8655

www.phillyseaport.org

CONTENTS

US CRUISERS 1883–1904
THE BIRTH OF THE STEEL NAVY

INTRODUCTION

The modern US Navy, with nuclear-powered aircraft carriers and submarines and Aegis cruisers with high-technology combat and communication systems stands in stark contrast to the US Navy as it existed at the beginning of 1883. At that time, the US Navy comprised antiquated wooden hulks and was outclassed by 12 other nations. The authorization of the all-steel cruisers, *Atlanta*, *Boston*, and *Chicago*, on March 3, 1883, marked not only a change in material for warship construction but also the beginning of a change in US naval strategy, and the first stirrings of an expansionary foreign policy.

From 1883 to 1904, 39 cruisers were authorized, providing the crucial impetus to the US steel and shipbuilding industries to invest in the new technologies necessary to build a modern steel navy. US cruisers figured prominently in the two naval victories of the 1898 Spanish-American War, with America acquiring a string of new territorial possessions in the Caribbean and Pacific. Thus, the design and development of these cruisers marked the emergence of the US as a global naval power.

A NAVAL RENAISSANCE

At the conclusion of the American Civil War in April 1865, the US Navy was one of the largest navies in the world, with a fleet in excess of 600 ships. More importantly, it was the most technologically advanced navy. Over the preceding years, the US Navy had been the first to introduce steam engines and the screw propeller and the first to eliminate sails on a steamship. The commissioning of the USS *Monitor* in February 1862 introduced armored revolving gun turrets on a ship's centerline, revolutionizing warship design. USS *Wampanoag* was the fastest steamship in the world in 1868.

However, during the post-1865 period, the US Navy gave up its technological leadership. In 1870, Navy regulations forbade the use of steam power. In 1874 it stopped ordering new warships. By 1881, the Navy comprised 26 operational ships, only four of which had iron hulls.

The coming of peace in 1865 allowed the United States to refocus its national efforts on Manifest Destiny, the settling of the West, and to develop the US's agricultural, mineral, and industrial resources. Waves of immigrants helped fuel the rapid expansion of the US economy. In 1874, US exports exceeded imports by value for the first time, reflecting the global emergence of US manufacturing capability. Reconstruction of the South was finished. By 1880,

OPPOSITE
USS *Atlanta* and *Boston*, showing their combination of sail power and steam power. This mix was necessary to give the ships the cruising range in a time of low-powered steam engines and the absence of overseas coaling stations.

government debts incurred for the Civil War had been significantly reduced, and the federal government enjoyed a solid budget surplus.

This growing economic strength sparked a national debate on the need for both an army and a navy. European imperialism was seeking new markets and territories in Africa, Asia, and the Pacific. Recognition that countries with significantly smaller economies were acquiring powerful, modern warships that could readily defeat any ship the US Navy possessed forced the administration of President Chester Arthur to act. In November 1881, Secretary of the Navy William Hunt advised both the President and the US Congress that, "The condition of the navy imperatively demands the prompt and earnest attention of Congress – or – it must soon dwindle into insignificance."

A key element in the national debate was provided by Theodore Roosevelt's book *The Naval War of 1812*, published in early 1882. Roosevelt identified that the United States won the War of 1812 because its navy was efficient and technically advanced. Roosevelt stated, "It is folly for the Republic to rely for defense upon a navy composed partly of antiquated hulks, and partly on new vessels rather more worthless than the old."

After significant political and public debate, as well as detailed reports submitted by two Naval Advisory Boards, new Secretary of the Navy William Chandler finally obtained Congressional approval for the construction of four new ships, all to be built from steel. Three ships, the USS *Atlanta*, *Boston*, and *Chicago*, were to be cruisers. The remaining ship, the USS *Dolphin*, was to be a dispatch vessel. These ships were referred to as the "ABCD ships," and they marked the birth of the new steel navy. The decision to build what were, in naval terms, three modest cruisers, had dramatic implications for the Navy, the shipbuilding industry, and, ultimately, America's role in world affairs.

In addition to obtaining Congress's approval for the new steel ships, Secretary Chandler attacked the waste, inefficiency, and processes of the "old navy." Naval shipyards, fully manned but idle, were rationalized. Maintenance and repair programs on obsolete ships were stopped, forcing these ships to be scrapped. Reform of naval personnel policy commenced with 400 officers being retired.

With the decks cleared, Chandler turned to the future of the "new navy," and in 1884, established the Naval War College (NWC), the first post-graduate naval education establishment in the world. The NWC's function was to teach the principles of war to naval officers so that "with their deeper understanding of the tactics and strategy of war" they would be both captains of ships and captains of war, to paraphrase Winston Churchill's comment on the Royal Navy in 1914.

 EARLY CLASSES OF CRUISER

USS *Atlanta*

Although *Atlanta* and *Boston* were obsolete when commissioned, they provided valuable experience for the new navy. *Boston* fought at Manila Bay with Dewey and served until 1946.

USS *Chicago*

The *Chicago* suffered from the same design issues as the smaller *Atlanta* and *Boston*, but at 4,500 tons, she was over four times larger than the last iron ship built for the Navy. *Chicago* introduced twin screws, but her compound overhead beam engines protruding through her decks belied her otherwise modern innovations. For armor protection, she relied on a steel deck supported by coal bunkers. *Chicago* was heavily armed and much admired by other navies, and served until 1936.

USS *ATLANTA*

USS *CHICAGO*

USS *Boston* on her speed trials at Newport, Rhode Island. Authorized in 1883, problems with steel quality and new construction methods delayed her commissioning until May 1887. *Boston* participated in the battle of Manila Bay.

The establishment of the NWC followed the establishment of the Office of Naval Intelligence (ONI) in 1882. The ONI's function was to collect and evaluate military and naval information from abroad, through its overseas naval attachés, and to undertake strategic planning for the Navy. With ONI and the NWC, the new navy had the intellectual and informational resources and the time to study, consider, and plan for the future.

The NWC played a major contributing role to the debate on the importance of seapower with the 1890 publication of Alfred Mahan's *The Influence of Sea Power Upon History, 1660–1783*, which established a battle fleet as a prerequisite for gaining command of the sea. Mahan had been appointed to the NWC in 1885, and his book was based upon a series of lectures he had given at the NWC.

American naval strategy in 1883 was based on coastal defense and commerce raiding. The ABC cruisers were approved within this context, with the additional element of "showing the flag," particularly in the Pacific, to support growing US commercial interests. The debate questioned the viability of a coastal defense and commerce-raiding strategy when the range of new naval guns outranged the guns on unseaworthy coastal defense monitors. Additionally, an effective commerce-raiding strategy would require a large number of cruisers scouring the seas to interdict enemy merchant shipping. This in turn raised the issue of the need for a fleet that could defend the US coast by defeating at sea an attacking naval force. This debate took many years to mature, and during this period, the new navy had to come to grips with more practical issues.

DESIGN AND CONSTRUCTION

The development of the new navy was determined by the development of the design and construction capabilities of American shipbuilders and the production capabilities of American steelmakers. The decay of the US Navy from 1866 to 1883 had resulted in a decline in the American naval shipbuilding industry to the point that no US Navy yard was capable of building steel ships.

Only two private shipyards, John Roach & Sons of Chester, Pennsylvania, and William Cramp & Sons of Philadelphia, Pennsylvania, bid on the contracts to build the three cruisers and the dispatch vessel. Roach won the contract to build all four ships. Technical problems in fabricating steel plates and casting large steel forgings for the propeller shafts, plus constant changes to design plans and specifications, slowed construction. Political interference resulted in the contracts with Roach being invalidated by the US government, forcing Roach into bankruptcy. As US Navy yards could not complete the ships, the US Navy assumed control of Roach's shipyards until the ships were completed.

William Cramp won the contracts for the next generation of cruisers, and the firm invested in new hydraulic tools to produce shaped hull plates and more powerful ships' boilers. A key feature in the development of US shipbuilding expertise was the acquisition by the US Navy of ship designs, including engine drawings from Armstrong of England, a leader in naval technology and design. The detailed plans for the triple-expansion steam engine, which was a major technological improvement over compound steam engines, enabled William Cramp to build more powerful engines in less space and to increase the speed of the ship.

Construction of steel ships was frustrated by the absence of production facilities for large quantities of high-quality steel and rolling mills that could shape steel plate to the curves of a ship's hull. Additionally, the standards set by the US Navy for steel were higher than those set by the British Admiralty for their warships and by Lloyds of London for insurable ships.

Although the US steel industry had expanded rapidly to meet the demand from US railroad, industrial, and mining growth, the steel required was mild steel and not the hard steel needed for warships. Heavy forgings of steel needed for engines and guns larger than 6in. were only available from overseas steelmakers. In 1885, Bethlehem Steel started the process to install open hearth steelmaking capability that would provide both the armor plate and heavy forgings for propeller shafts, engines, and guns. Bethlehem purchased a steel-manufacturing plant from Whitworth in England. This plant had to be shipped to the United States and assembled. It was 1888 before the quality and quantity of steel needed by the US Navy could be supplied.

A 6-in. gun on *Boston*'s midship gun deck. Built before gun training and hydraulic power were developed, the gun carriage relied on a gravity slide to manage gun recoil and on deck slides with worm gear for training the gun.

The Navy established a manufacturing plant for rifled breech-loading guns at the Washington Navy Yard in 1882. Using steel forgings from the Midvale Steel Company of Philadelphia, which supplied the structural steel shapes for the Brooklyn Bridge, the Navy was able to produce 6in. and smaller guns for the new steel cruisers. In 1886, the Washington Navy Yard was designated the manufacturing center for all naval ordnance, and Congress stipulated that the material for all new ships had to be manufactured domestically.

In 1887, the Navy combined their steel requirements for high-quality steel, armor plate, and engine and gun forgings into large contracts to provide the incentive for steelmakers to invest in the technology and plants needed to meet this demand. Bethlehem Steel bid and won contracts for 6,700 tons of armor plate and 1,300 tons

The Squadron of Evolution at anchor off Newport, Rhode Island, in 1889. The photograph shows *Chicago*, with *Atlanta* and *Boston* anchored astern and the gunboat *Yorktown* in the far distance. Working with the NWC, this squadron undertook the first fleet exercises for the new navy.

of gun forgings. However, there were considerable delays in the performance of the contract due to technical issues. In 1891, Carnegie Steel agreed to manufacture armor plate, and they produced the first nickel-steel armor plate in the United States.

The period from 1886 to 1902 was marked by significant frustration and delays as US steelmakers perfected production techniques for armor plate to meet the US Navy's exacting standards. Agreement between the Navy and armor plate producers on pricing was a major political and contractual issue throughout this period, complicated by new types of armor plate being invented by Schneider of France, Harvey of the United States, and Krupp of Germany. The new armor required changing production techniques, sourcing new minerals, and agreeing to royalties with the inventor.

In 1902, Charles Schwab, president of Carnegie Steel, commented that the ABC cruisers had provided the practical beginnings for the successful manufacture of structural steel in America. In addition to new steel ships, city skylines began to change, as new buildings built with steel frames climbed skyward, to be named "skyscrapers."

Boston's teak chart house, showing the telegraph, binnacle, and wheel. The heating coils and armchair, shown to the left of the photograph, provided a minimal level of comfort.

THE SHIPS

Congress authorized and allocated funds for the construction of naval ships in the annual government budget process. The following section outlines the development of those ships authorized from 1883 to 1904.

Ships authorized in 1883

In matching the design of the ABC cruisers to their role of showing the flag in far-flung locations and commerce raiding, designers had to find the balance between speed, endurance, armament, and protection, within a specified displacement, hull size, and shipbuilding capability.

The lack of overseas coaling stations and the unreliability of heavily vibrating reciprocating steam engines required auxiliary sail power to provide transoceanic patrolling endurance. The weight of masts and yards ate into the other elements of the design, and the final compromised result invited strong criticism.

The largest cruiser, USS *Chicago*, enjoyed a heavier armament of four 8-in., eight 6-in., and two 5-in. guns. The 8-in. guns were positioned in sponsons on beams, forward and aft, providing strong end-on-end fire, an important feature for running down and overwhelming enemy shipping. As a result, the *Chicago* was one of the more powerful cruisers of her day. *Chicago* also enjoyed twin screws, a new feature for US Navy ships. However, this was compromised by an overhead beam engine and cylindrical boilers placed over brick fireboxes that were a technological throwback to early industrial steam engines.

The final designs for the ABC cruisers were subsequently seen as poor. The ships were not balanced between engine power and hull shape. The designs were hampered by sailing rig that compromised steam power to the extent that the cruisers lacked the speed for commerce raiding. Armaments for USS *Atlanta* and *Boston* were seen as insufficient, and the ships lacked armor and had to rely on coal bunkers for protection.

Although the design of the ABC cruisers was criticized, and the 8-in. breech-loading guns had to be supplied from Britain, they nevertheless provided the breakthrough in skills and experience needed to build the next

USS *Chicago*: larger than the *Atlanta* and *Boston*, she took six years to build, before being commissioned in 1889. Although powered by outdated steam engines, she carried a powerful mix of armaments for her day, and was admired by European navies.

set of cruisers. The ABC ships had double bottoms, watertight compartments, and electric power plants as standard auxiliary equipment. These features alone represented major design developments for the US Navy.

Name	Builder	Launched	Commissioned
Atlanta	John Roach	October 9, 1884	July 19, 1886
Boston	John Roach	December 4, 1884	May 2, 1887
Chicago	John Roach	December 5, 1885	April 17, 1889

Ships authorized in 1885

In March 1885, two additional cruisers were authorized, USS *Newark* and *Charleston*. *Newark* represented a significant step forward in design. The protective deck was extended to cover the entire length of the hull, and therefore classified the ship as a protected cruiser. A horizontal triple-expansion engine powered her to 19 knots, a four-knot increase over the earlier cruisers. This rebalance in design required that she be armed with a homogeneous set of 12 6-in. guns, rather than carry the weight of the far heavier 8-in. guns. However, the *Newark* still carried a full set of sails.

Frustration over design issues resulted in the US Navy buying a set of building plans for the *Charleston* from the Armstrong shipyards in Britain. At that time, Armstrong was building cruisers for many nations at its Elswick shipyards. Secretary of the Navy William C. Whitney used the acquisition of foreign designs to spur on Congress for the development of domestic shipbuilding capabilities.

The *Charleston* was the first major steel warship to be built by the Union Iron Works of San Francisco, California. This development gave the US Navy a shipbuilding capability on both the Atlantic and Pacific coasts, which was important in the period before the Panama Canal was constructed. The *Charleston* was armed with two 8-in. guns mounted fore and aft and six 6-in. guns mounted on either beam, with a protective deck covering the full hull length.

USS *Newark* coaling, 1898. The first cruiser to be built by William Cramp in Philadelphia, it represented a major development in cruiser design with a full protective deck, triple-expansion engines, and torpedo tubes.

Name	Builder	Launched	Commissioned
Newark	William Cramp	March 19, 1890	February 2, 1891
Charleston	Union Iron Works	July 19, 1888	December 26, 1889

Ships authorized in 1886

In 1886, another protected cruiser was authorized, again using plans bought from Armstrong. This ship, the USS *Baltimore*, became the first ship of the new navy to be built without sail power. The horizontal triple-expansion engines produced 10,000 horsepower (hp), and, matched to her hull, produced a speed of just under 20 knots. The *Baltimore* carried a main armament of four 8-in. guns in sponsons on her forecastle and aft deck with six 6-in. guns mounted in sponsons on either beam.

In addition to the *Baltimore*, Congress approved two armored cruisers with a displacement of 6,000 tons each. This approval was part of the strategy to promote the further development of US shipbuilding, particularly at US Navy shipyards. This was done by Congress responding to Secretary Whitney by requiring that the steel and machinery for these ships was to be sourced solely from US manufacturers. Both ships were built in US Navy yards.

The two ships became the USS *Texas* and *Maine* and were reclassified during their construction as second-class battleships. Both ships experienced significant delays during construction, one reason being the time needed to manufacture their armor plate. These ships were commissioned in 1895, nine years after being authorized.

USS *Baltimore* in New York harbor, 1903. Another Armstrong-designed cruiser, the *Baltimore* was the first US cruiser to be built without sails. *Baltimore* participated in the battle of Manila Bay and laid the North Sea mine barrage from 1917 to 1918.

Name	Builder	Launched	Commissioned
Baltimore	William Cramp	October 6, 1888	January 7, 1890

Ships authorized in 1887

Two protected cruisers were authorized in 1887, the USS *Philadelphia* and *San Francisco*. Both ships closely followed their predecessors. The *Philadelphia* was a near copy of the *Baltimore*, but carried a homogeneous main armament of 12 6-in. guns. Fore and aft sails were carried on all three masts. The *San Francisco* followed the plans for the *Newark*, but the positions for her guns were located on her fore and aft decks rather than in sponsons. The *San Francisco* carried a schooner rig.

In addition to the ABC cruisers, the US Navy had, by the end of 1887, five protected cruisers under construction and two cruisers in commission. During the prior four years, the Navy had increased the speed of its ships by five knots, eliminated sails on one of its ships, standardized armament, introduced electricity as standard auxiliary equipment, and had two major shipyards, William Cramp and Union Iron Works, capable of building steel warships. The Washington Navy Yard was now able to manufacture guns with bores of up to 12in.

USS *San Francisco* dressed with flags. Considered the most successful of the early protected cruisers, the positioning of her armament on the upper decks gave strong end-on-end fire. Built under a fixed-price contract with performance incentives, *San Francisco* exceeded her contracted speed specification.

Name	Builder	Launched	Commissioned
Philadelphia	William Cramp	September 7, 1889	July 28, 1890
San Francisco	Union Iron Works	August 14, 1889	November 15, 1890

Ships authorized in 1888

Three classes of cruiser were approved in 1888, with a total of seven ships authorized: three protected cruisers with advanced armament and engines, three unprotected cruisers, and the first armored cruiser.

There was a further categorization within the three protected cruisers. One was to be larger than those authorized to date, the other two to be limited to a displacement of

B USS OLYMPIA

Olympia was the only US protected cruiser to carry her main armament in armored turrets. Intriguingly, *Olympia* suffered a series of spontaneous coal bunker fires during her initial voyage to Japan. One fire was in a bunker adjacent to a magazine and melted the lead joins in the bulkhead. Please note that the officer's wardroom has been repositioned for the purposes of this diagram, and would in fact have been located in the superstructure just aft of the mainmast.

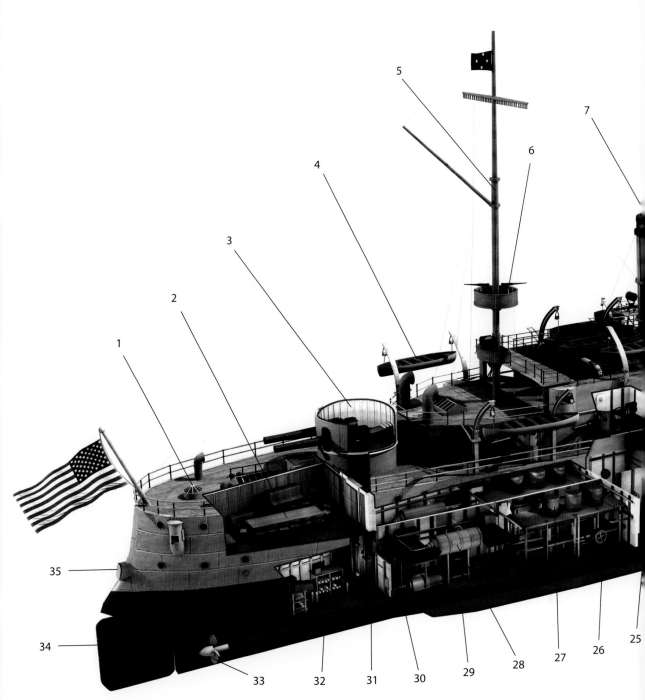

SPECIFICATIONS – *OLYMPIA*

Displacement: 5,870 tons

Waterline load length: 340ft

Beam: 53ft ⅝ in.

Armament: 4 x 8-in./.35-cal.; 10 x 5-in./.40-cal.; 14 x 6pdr; 6 x 1pdr; 4 Gatlings

Crew: 33 officers, 395 enlisted men

KEY

1 Skylight
2 Officer's wardroom
3 Aft 8-in. gun turret
4 Port 32ft whaleboat
5 Mainmast
6 Fighting top with two 1pdr quick-firing guns
7 Aft funnel
8 Ship's boats
9 Cowl vent
10 Forward funnel
11 Teak pilot house
12 Foremast
13 Fighting top with 1pdr quick-firing gun
14 Searchlight
15 Forward bridge deck
16 Forward 8-in. gun turret
17 Anchor davits
18 Bow torpedo tube
19 Anchor
20 Conning tower
21 Driggs-Schroeder 6pdr quick-firing gun
22 Coal bunker
23 Double stoked boiler
24 5-in. gun
25 Fire room
26 Engine controls
27 Engine cylinder head
28 Condenser
29 Propeller shaft
30 Longitudinal bulkhead dividing port and starboard engine and boiler rooms
31 8-in. ammunition hoist within armored tube
32 8-in. aft magazine
33 Starboard propellor
34 Rudder
35 Aft torpedo tube

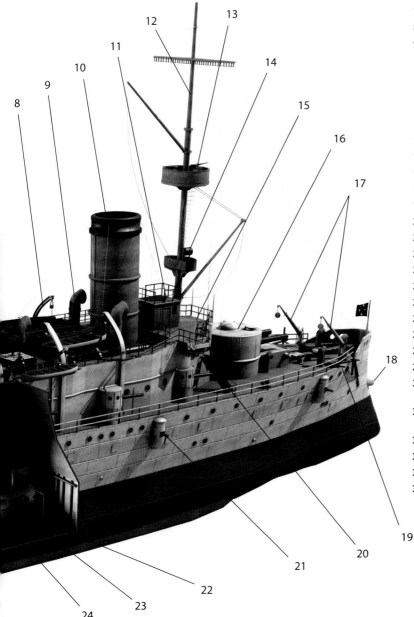

USS *Philadelphia* in 1892. Built by William Cramp shipyards, *Philadelphia* was a copy of the *Baltimore*, but her high freeboard, coupled with the armament positioned on the forecastle and quarterdeck, resulted in a lack of stability and the need to carry ballast.

3,000 tons. The larger ship became the USS *Olympia*. The increased hull dimensions allowed the *Olympia* to be fitted with vertical triple-expansion engines, rather than horizontal. The increased engine power enabled the ship to exceed 21 knots. Additionally, her armament of four 8-in. guns carried in two turrets and ten 5-in. guns in beam casemates was a very efficient and powerful arrangement.

The two smaller protected cruisers, USS *Cincinnati* and *Raleigh*, proved to be a less successful design. Although they were able to reach 19 knots, the small hull with powerful engines resulted in poor ventilation and excess temperatures within her machine and boiler rooms. The crews of these ships were not able to work regular shifts in 200-degree Fahrenheit heat.

The unprotected cruisers were effectively enlarged gunboats. Able to work in shallow waters, they were soon seen as "peace cruisers," showing the flag but unable to meet wartime requirements. These ships were the USS *Montgomery*, *Detroit*, and *Marblehead*.

The USS *New York* was the Navy's first armored cruiser. Modeled on the original French design for the *Dupuy de Lome*, the *New York* was fitted with a belt of 4-in. compound armor plate in addition to the protected deck. With four vertical triple-expansion engines producing 17,000hp, the *New York* exceeded 21 knots. Two of her engines could be decoupled for economic cruising. The ship had to stop for the two engines to be recoupled when full speed was required, a key factor during the battle of Santiago. *New York*'s armament of six 8-in. guns and 12 4-in. guns was not thought to be well balanced because the 4-in. gun was unwieldy, unable to inflict serious damage on an armored adversary, and too slow to be able to ward off torpedo boats. *New York* was laid down at William Cramp's shipyard in 1890 and commissioned in 1893, representing an improvement in construction time for what was the Navy's largest and most complicated warship to date.

The successful domestic design and construction of the *Olympia* and *New York* marked the capability of US naval designers and the US shipbuilding industry to design and build modern warships that equaled and/or outclassed foreign warships.

USS *Cincinnati* was designed as a small, fast, protected cruiser, and was the first cruiser built at the New York Navy Yard. Her powerful engines and boilers cramped the ship and limited her range of operation.

The inauguration of President Benjamin Harrison in March 1889 provided additional impetus in the development of the new steel navy. President Harrison called for further expansion of the Navy and the acquisition of overseas naval bases. A new Secretary of the Navy, Benjamin Tracy, supported the growing realization that the US Navy needed a battle fleet to "meet and vanquish" an enemy "before he has sighted our coast," as stated by Admiral Philip Hichborn. The authorization of the USS *Texas*, *Maine*, and the armored cruiser *New York*, reflected a growing awareness of the need for armored ships, and for industry to produce armor plate. Tracy ordered the ABC cruisers to be formed into the Squadron of Evolution. This squadron conducted the first fleet exercises of the US Navy, and marked the beginning of the evolution in officer training from single-ship cruiser engagements to battle-line fleet engagements. The NWC, using its Strategic War Game scenarios, established fleet doctrine, and, with the Squadron of Evolution, developed fleet/squadron tactics and communications.

Name	Builder	Launched	Commissioned
Olympia	Union Iron Works	November 5, 1892	February 5, 1895
Cincinnati	New York Navy Yard	November 10, 1892	June 16, 1894
Raleigh	Norfolk Navy Yard	March 31, 1892	April 17,1894
Montgomery	Columbian Iron Works	December 5, 1891	June 21, 1894
Detroit	Columbian Iron Works	October 28, 1891	July 20, 1893
Marblehead	City Point Works	August 11, 1892	April 2, 1894
New York	William Cramp	December 2, 1891	August 1, 1893

USS *Columbia* in 1898. She was designed as a fast commerce raider, specifically to catch fast ocean liners converted to armed raiders. *Columbia's* comparative lack of heavy armament reduced her service life as the Navy's strategy moved to command of the sea.

Ships authorized from 1890 to 1891

Only one cruiser was authorized in 1890, the USS *Columbia*. This ship and her sister ship, the USS *Minneapolis*, authorized in 1891, were enlarged *Olympia*s. The increased hull length allowed three engines to be fitted, each linked to its own propeller. This gave the ships a speed of 23 knots and an ability to use only the central engine and propeller for economical cruising. The role of these ships was commerce raiding, and they possessed the speed to catch and overwhelm converted, armed liners. The success of their design was demonstrated when the *Columbia* outraced the German Hamburg liner *Augusta-Victoria* across the Atlantic in 1895, setting a record at just under seven days. *Minneapolis* and *Columbia* marked the end of protected cruiser construction and reliance on a commerce-raiding strategy

1890, like 1883, was a pivotal year for the US Navy. The maturing of the debate on naval strategy reflected on the growth of Germany, Italy, and Japan as naval powers. Additionally, Great Britain had passed the Naval Defence Act of 1889, establishing a two-navy standard, and had authorized construction of ten battleships and 42 cruisers. The naval building programs of France and Russia reflected the importance of battleships.

The publication of Mahan's *The Influence of Sea Power Upon History, 1660–1783* provided a historical context on the need for a battle fleet to achieve command of the sea. The building of the steel cruisers had provided the experience needed to design and build modern steel warships. Steelmakers had invested in new plants to manufacture armor plate and to supply the forgings for the manufacture of heavy guns. In 1890, the Washington Navy Yard conducted a test to determine which of the types of armor plate provided the best protection. An alloy of nickel and steel proved to be the strongest, and the following year, August Harvey, an American, invented a hardening process for this new alloy.

As Secretary Chandler had before him, Secretary Tracy appointed a policy board to recommend a fleet structure. This board recommended a two-ocean fleet with 35 battleships and 24 armored cruisers. As importantly, the policy board advocated a naval strategy for command of the sea approaches to the United States. The role of cruisers was detailed as "working as part of an integrated fleet" as well as commerce raiding. The ensuing political debate accepted the need for battleships and a new naval strategy. Three battleships, the USS *Indiana, Massachusetts*, and *Oregon*, were approved in 1890.

In April 1891, Tracy announced a new administrative policy for US Navy yards that removed hiring and firing from political patronage to a government-codified meritocracy. This critical development reflected frustration with the delays in the construction of the *Maine* and *Texas*.

Name	Builder	Launched	Commissioned
Columbia	William Cramp	July 26, 1892	April 23, 1894
Minneapolis	William Cramp	August 12, 1892	December 13, 1894

Ships authorized in 1892

The political debate that resulted in the authorization of the three battleships had taken place during an economic depression. A midterm election in 1890 changed the political balance of Congress, and, in the ensuing debate, only one battleship, USS *Iowa*, and one armored cruiser, USS *Brooklyn*, were authorized in 1892.

The USS *Brooklyn* was an enlarged *New York*. The longer hull and increased efficiency of her boilers made her one knot faster than the *New York*. The design for the *Brooklyn* drew upon a French design feature, a tumblehome for her sides that allowed beam turrets to be trained from dead ahead to dead astern. With eight 8-in. guns in four turrets and 12 5-in. rapid fire guns, the *Brooklyn* had a far more effective armament than the *New York*. A further significant feature of the *Brooklyn* was her armored belt. This comprised 3in. of the new Harvey nickel armor, which was stronger than the 4-in. compound armor of the *New York*.

The *Brooklyn* also served as test bed for a competition between new electric-powered turret training machinery in two 8-in. gun turrets and the established steam-powered system in the remaining two turrets. The electric-powered system proved to be superior and was adopted on later warships.

Name	Builder	Launched	Commissioned
Brooklyn	William Cramp	October 2, 1895	December 1, 1896

Ships authorized from 1893 to 1898

During this six-year period, only battleships were authorized. They were the USS *Kersage*, *Illinois*, *Alabama*, *Wisconsin*, *Maine*, and *Ohio*. However, 11 cruisers were commissioned during the same period.

In April 1897, Theodore Roosevelt was appointed Under Secretary of the Navy, supporting Secretary John Long. That September, Roosevelt proposed building six new armored cruisers similar to the *Brooklyn*, but with a heavier armament. Roosevelt was concerned by Japan's growing naval strength and German colonial aspirations in the Pacific. However, action on Roosevelt's proposal had to wait until after the Spanish-American War.

USS *Brooklyn* at the New York Navy Yard. An improved *New York* armored cruiser, she led the van during the battle of Santiago. Using a French design concept of tumblehome sides enabled her beam turrets to fire both fore and aft.

USS *New Orleans* in New York, April 1898. Built by Armstrong for Brazil and purchased as part of the "Fifty Million Dollar Bill," the *New Orleans* formed part of the Cuban blockade during the Spanish-American War.

In early 1898, prior to the war with Spain, the US Navy bought two cruisers from Brazil in an attempt to increase the size of her fleet and to deny Spain the opportunity to acquire new warships. Both ships were nearing completion at the Armstrong shipyards in England. The acquisition of the two ships was completed on March 16, 1898. This followed Congressional passage of the emergency defense appropriation, the "Fifty Million Dollar Bill," which funded a rapid increase in the Navy for the anticipated war with Spain. The first ship was commissioned as the USS *Amazonas* and sailed from England for New York, where she was renamed the USS *New Orleans*, before sailing to join the squadron blockading Cuba. The second ship missed the war and was completed as the USS *Albany*.

America's success in the Spanish-American War brought home a number of important lessons. First, the United States needed a large navy. The cities on the East Coast had been left practically undefended when Admiral William Sampson concentrated his fleet in Key West, Florida. Secondly, the ability of the United States to be successful in future conflicts could only be achieved through fleet action, not commerce-destroying warfare. Finally, with two oceans lapping her shores, the US Navy needed ships with lengthy cruising ranges, offshore fueling bases, and a canal across Panama.

Name	Builder	Launched	Commissioned
New Orleans	Armstrong, Whitworth & Co., UK	December 4, 1896	March 18, 1898 as USS *Amazonas* (Renamed *New Orleans* on April15,1898)
Albany	Armstrong, Whitworth & Co., UK	January 14, 1899	May 29, 1900

Ships authorized in 1899

The success of the USS *Brooklyn* and *New York* during the Spanish-American War, and the building of the powerful Cressy class of armored cruisers for the Royal Navy provided a powerful incentive for Congress to authorize three armored cruisers in 1899.

The Pennsylvania class comprised the USS *Pennsylvania*, *West Virginia*, and *California*. These ships, at 13,680 tons, displaced 1,268 tons less than the Virginia-class battleships authorized in the same year, but were 67 feet longer. A battleship-sized complement was necessary to crew the large machinery and boiler rooms that produced in excess of 28,000hp to give a top speed of 22 knots. The speed was obtained in part by less weight in armor protection and a reduced level of armament, relative to battleships. The role of the armored cruiser was two-fold: to act as a fast wing of the battle fleet, and to engage as a commerce destroyer, particularly against fast, armed liners.

Victory in the Spanish-American War brought with it America's first major overseas colony, the Philippines. In addition, in 1899, America required that its Open Door policy be adopted by all nations trading with China in order to protect its own trade with that nation. Gunboats and peace cruisers able to navigate China's rivers were an important means for America to protect its interests in China. The Caribbean and South American waters also required the presence of US Navy ships.

In 1899, authorization was given for a further six peace cruisers of the Denver class: the USS *Denver*, *Des Moines*, *Chattanooga*, *Galveston*, *Tacoma*, and *Cleveland*. These ships were specifically designed for service in the tropics. The steel hulls were sheathed in wood and then finished with copper, to inhibit marine growth.

The construction of a number of these peace cruisers was undertaken by several shipyards that had not previously built warships for the US Navy. This was seen as a way to build up US naval shipbuilding infrastructure. However, two shipyards were unable to complete their contracts, and the USS *Chattanooga* and *Galveston* had to be completed in Navy yards.

Name	Builder	Launched	Commissioned
Pennsylvania	William Cramp	August 22, 1903	March 9, 1905
West Virginia	Newport News	April 18, 1903	February 23, 1905
California	Union Iron Works	April 28, 1904	August 1, 1907
Denver	Neafie & Levy	June 21, 1902	May 17, 1904
Des Moines	Fore River S. & E. Co.	September 20, 1903	March 5, 1904
Chattanooga	Crescent Shipyard/New York Navy Yard	March 7, 1903	October 11, 1904
Galveston	William R. Trigg/Norfolk Navy Yard	July 23, 1903	February 15, 1905
Tacoma	Union Iron Works	June 2, 1903	January 30, 1904
Cleveland	Bath Iron Works	September 28, 1901	November 2, 1903

USS *California* in 1908. She was a member of the Pennsylvania class of armored cruisers; renamed USS *San Diego* in September 1914, she was sunk in July 1918 by U-156 off Fire Island, New York.

USS *Denver*, October 1904. *Denver* was specifically built for service in the tropics because the US Navy needed additional peace cruisers to show the flag in overseas possessions following the Spanish-American War.

Ships authorized in 1900

The need for a strong squadron of armored cruisers resulted in a further six being authorized in 1900. Three of the new ships, the USS *Colorado*, *Maryland*, and *South Dakota*, were members of the Pennsylvania class and copied their design. The other three, the USS *St. Louis*, *Milwaukee*, and *Charleston*, were an unsuccessful design, and within five years were relegated to administrative duties. These ships were smaller than the Pennsylvania class. Their main armament was placed in open mounts and their reduced belt armor did not cover the complete hull length.

Secretary Long appointed Admiral George Dewey, the victor at the battle of Manila Bay, to head a new General Board of the Navy, which was to make "recommendations as to the proper disposition of the fleet." This board became, in effect, a general staff function and involved itself across a wide area of naval activities, particularly ship design and construction.

Name	Builder	Launched	Commissioned
Colorado	William Cramp	April 25, 1903	January 19, 1905
Maryland	Newport News	September 12, 1903	April 18, 1905
South Dakota	Union Iron works	July 21, 1904	January 27, 1908
St. Louis	Neafie & Levy	May 6, 1905	August 18, 1906
Milwaukee	Union Iron Work	September 10, 1904	December 11, 1906
Charleston	Newport News	January 23, 1904	October 17, 1905

Ships authorized from 1902 to 1904

In 1902 a new class of armored cruiser was authorized, the Tennessee class. These ships, the USS *Tennessee* and *Washington*, and two more authorized in 1904, the USS *North Carolina* and *Montana*, were the last armored cruisers to be built. These four ships were commissioned from 1906 to 1908,

LATER CLASSES OF CRUISER

USS *Olympia*

A side-profile and top-down view of the USS *Olympia*. *Olympia* was first authorized in 1888 and with her vertical triple-expansion engines she could exceed 21 knots.

USS *Tennessee*

Armored cruisers of the Tennessee class were the largest and the last armored cruisers built for the US Navy. The Tennessee class was more powerful than the Minotaur and Scharnhorst classes of armored cruiser built by Britain and Germany, respectively, and they were introduced at the same time as the Tennessee class. Additionally, they were more powerful than the *Nisshin* armored cruisers of Japan, their most likely opponent in a naval conflict.

USS *OLYMPIA*

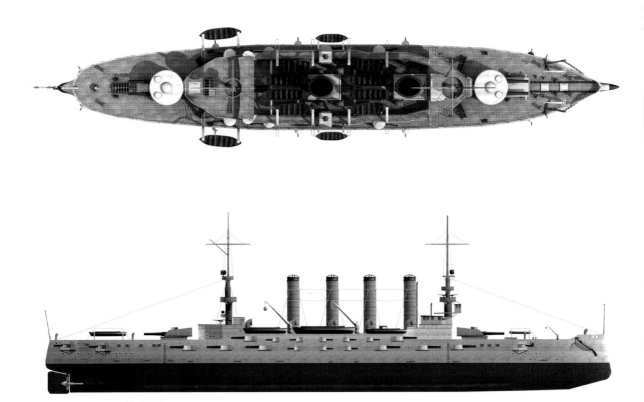

USS *TENNESSEE*

coinciding with the laying down and launching of the first battle cruisers for the Royal Navy, whose speed and armament exceeded any armored cruiser afloat.

The Tennessee-class ships carried a heavy armament of four 10-in. and 16 6-in. guns and were capable of a top speed of 22 knots. The Pennsylvania and the Tennessee class of armored cruisers responded to Roosevelt's 1897 proposal and were designed to provide a fast and powerful initial response to Japanese battleships in the eventuality of a Pacific war. US battleships would need time to sail from the Atlantic around South America to the Pacific, and the armored cruisers provided an advance guard for West Coast United States defense.

Japan's naval might was clearly demonstrated in 1905 when Admiral Togo's fleet of battleships and armored cruisers inflicted a crushing defeat on the Russian fleet at the battle of the Sea of Japan. As a result, the NWC began to formulate plans for a war with Japan that became known as Plan Orange.

Under President Theodore Roosevelt, the new navy came of age. In December 1907, 16 battleships of the US Navy set sail to circumnavigate the world. The US Navy was now the second most powerful navy in the world, and the voyage of the Great White Fleet, as the white-painted battleships were referred to, demonstrated this fact.

The Great White Fleet joined with the eight armored cruisers of the new US Pacific Fleet, formed from the Asiatic Squadron, in San Francisco Bay on May 5, 1908. It represented the largest fleet of warships that had sailed the Pacific.

The cruisers of the period from 1883 to 1904 period provided sterling service throughout their careers. The armored cruisers, in particular, served throughout the two years of American involvement in World War I, providing convoy protection and carrying US troops to and from Europe. Only the *California*, renamed *San Diego*, was lost to enemy action, in July 1918. It was sunk by U-156 off Fire Island, New York. As the US Navy increased in size and in types of ship, ship names were structured relating battleships to states and armored cruisers to cities.

Name	Builder	Launched	Commissioned
Tennessee	William Cramp	December 3, 1904	July 17, 1906
Washington	New York Shipbuilding	March 18, 1905	August 7, 1906
North Carolina	Newport News	October 6, 1906	May 7, 1908
Montana	Newport News	December 15, 1906	July 21, 1908

CRUISERS IN ACTION

The Spanish-American War, 1898

The origins of the Spanish-American War lay in American support for the independence of Cuba from Spain. Spain's brutal suppression of Cuban insurgents horrified the American public. The US government sought a diplomatic solution, but the explosion and sinking of the USS *Maine* in Havana harbor on February 15, 1898, while on a goodwill mission, made a successful diplomatic outcome problematic. President William McKinley ordered the US Navy to blockade Cuba on April 21, and Congress declared war on April 24.

The US Navy had started planning for a war with Spain in 1895, when the NWC began an exercise to identify the options available to the Navy. These options were seen as: a direct attack on Spain; an attack on Spain's Pacific colonies of the Philippines and Guam; or an attack on Spain's colonies in the Caribbean, Cuba, and Puerto Rico. Over the next several years, the options were reworked with input from ONI and reviews by a planning board that reported to the Secretary of the Navy. In this process, the first option of a direct attack on Spain was ruled out.

Admiral Sampson, commanding the North Atlantic Squadron based at Key West, commenced a blockade of Cuba on April 22. This blockade was intended to deny supplies to Spanish forces and to force the Spanish government into sending a naval force to lift the blockade. However, before Spanish forces arrived in the Caribbean to attempt to lift the blockade, Commodore Dewey and his cruisers sailed into Manila Bay in the Philippines.

The battle of Manila Bay

In October 1897, Under Secretary of the Navy Theodore Roosevelt managed to have Commodore Dewey appointed to command the Asiatic Squadron in anticipation of war with Spain. Dewey had earned the reputation of being dynamic, and he had Civil War naval battle experience, having served under Admiral David Farragut of "Damn the torpedoes – full speed ahead!" fame. Dewey's reputation appealed to Roosevelt, who had a similar temperament.

The USS *Pennsylvania* was renamed USS *Pittsburg* in August 1912, and is shown here in dry dock in Brazil. In 1911, Eugene Ely made aviation history by landing an aircraft on *Pennsylvania* and then taking off.

USS *Maryland* on the target range in Manila Bay, showing the forward gun turret and superstructure, with a range finder visible on a platform on the forward mast. The supports for the two semaphore stations on the bridge wings are also visible.

Before leaving Washington, D.C., to take up his command, Dewey began the detailed planning for action in the Philippines. He joined his flagship, USS *Olympia*, in Nagasaki, Japan, and then sailed to Hong Kong.

On February 25, 1898, in the middle of the *Maine* crisis, Roosevelt cabled Dewey in Hong Kong, instructing, "Order the squadron except *Monocacy* to Hong Kong. Keep full of coal. In the event of war with Spain, your duty will be to see that the Spanish squadron does not leave the Asiatic coast and then offensive operations in the Philippine islands. Keep *Olympia* until further orders."

The USS *Monocacy* was an "old navy" wooden paddle wheeler. The last element of the cable was critical for Dewey because the *Olympia* was due to return to the United States, to be replaced by the USS *Baltimore*. This ship arrived in Hong Kong on April 21, carrying supplies of ammunition ordered by Dewey while he was in Washington.

On April 23, the Acting Governor of Hong Kong, General Wilsone Black, proclaimed Hong Kong neutral in the war between America and Spain, requesting that the American squadron leave Hong Kong by 4:00pm on April 25. Dewey protested because Congress had not yet formally declared war. However, the deadline stood. On April 24, Secretary of the Navy Long cabled Dewey in Hong Kong, advising, "War has commenced between United States and Spain. Proceed at once to Philippine Islands. Commence operations at once, particularly against Spanish fleet. You must capture vessels or destroy. Use utmost endeavors."

Dewey's squadron left Hong Kong and anchored in Mirs Bay on the China coast. There he awaited the arrival from Manila of US Consul to the Philippines Oscar Williams, who, on April 27, brought with him a Philippine insurgent, Chief Alijandrini. Consul Williams detailed the latest information on the disposition of Spanish forces at a conference with Dewey, his staff, and captains on board *Olympia* at approximately midday. The squadron then sailed from Mirs Bay for Manila at 2:00pm that day. As the ships sailed toward Manila, they left in their wake wooden fittings, thrown overboard to decrease the risk of onboard fires during battle.

Dewey's squadron included four cruisers: the *Olympia*, *Boston*, *Baltimore*, and *Raleigh*; two gunboats, the *Petrel* and *Concord*; the armed revenue cutter *McCulloch*; and two unarmed supply ships, *Nanshan* and *Zafiro* – an embryonic Pacific fleet train. Dewey's force was stronger than the Spanish squadron under Admiral Patricio Montojo, which comprised

D **USS *OLYMPIA*, HONG KONG, 1898**
This painting of *Olympia* shows her on April 19, 1898, in Hong Kong harbor, being painted war gray over her white Asiatic colors. Cargo sampans are bringing and loading coal in preparation for the voyage to Manila. After the battle, Admiral Dewey stated, "The Battle of Manila Bay was fought in Hong Kong. That is, the hard work was done there; the execution here was not difficult ... my plans were carefully studied out there and no detail omitted."

D USS *OLYMPIA*, HONG KONG, 1898

Admiral Dewey, in his tropical uniform, standing on the forward deck of *Olympia*. Promoted to Admiral of the Navy by Congress after his victory at Manila Bay, Dewey became President of the General Board of the Navy.

seven ships: two old, unarmored cruisers, *Reina Cristina* and *Castilla*; four torpedo gunboats, *Isla de Cuba*, *Isla de Luzon*, *Don Antonio de Ulloa*, and *Don Juan de Austria*; and a gunboat, *Marques del Duero*.

Dewey had ten 8-in, 23 6-in., and 20 5-in. guns among his ships, while Admiral Montojo had seven 6.2-in., four 5.9-in., 30 4.7-in., and three 3.4-in. guns. However, Admiral Montojo had a further 23 gunboats, some armed with torpedoes, whose whereabouts were unknown. In addition, according to Consul Williams, there were coastal defense batteries guarding Manila City: the naval bases at Cavite and Sangley Point, all within Manila Bay, and at the two narrow entrances to Manila Bay itself. Additionally, the entrances to Manila Bay and the approaches to Cavite were mined. Combined, the Spanish squadron, coastal batteries, mines, and torpedo boats represented a powerful defensive force. Although Dewey's ships were heavily armed, they were vulnerable in respect to their thin armor. Furthermore, the US vessels were 7,000 miles from base, repairs, reinforcements, and supplies, particularly coal and ammunition.

An outstanding feature of the battle of Manila Bay is Dewey's aggressive confidence in tackling the Spanish squadron and its supporting coastal defenses. At 5:30pm on April 30, 1898, off the entrance to Manila Bay, Dewey called for his captains to join him on board *Olympia*. During this meeting, Dewey detailed his plan to enter Manila Bay at night, in single column with *Olympia* in the lead. They would use the Boca Grande channel rather than the main shipping channel of Boca Chica, to avoid the gun batteries on Corregidor Island that commanded this channel. Boca Grande was a more hazardous channel to navigate and was mined. Dewey explained to his captains that, as the channel was deeper than Boca Chica, it was more difficult for the mines to be set at the correct depth to make them a significant danger. In addition, warm tropical water quickly corrodes underwater mines. When someone pointed out that the first ship might set off the mines, Dewey demonstrated Farragut's attitude of "Damn the torpedoes" by stating that mines or no mines, "I am leading the squadron in myself." The new navy was benefiting from the old navy's aggressive war experience.

At 11pm, *Olympia* entered the Boca Grande channel with only outdated navigational charts to assist them. Behind *Olympia* steamed *Baltimore*, *Raleigh*, *Petrel*, *Concord*, *Boston*, *McCulloch*, *Nanshan*, and *Zafiro*. Each ship was blacked out, except for a single shaded white light at the stern as a guide for the following ship. All guns were loaded but the breeches left open to prevent accidental firing.

The Boca Grande channel was guarded by 17 guns, six being rapid-fire 4.7-in. located on the island of El Fraile that formed the southern section of the channel. At 12:15am on May 1, the battery on El Fraile opened fire, as *McCulloch* had revealed herself by flames shooting out from her smokestack. The shells fell between *Raleigh* and *Petrel*, which returned fire along with *Boston* and *Concord*. The battery ceased fire.

Upon entering the bay, Dewey slowed his squadron to four knots to time his arrival off Manila City, 24 miles away, at daybreak, where he expected to meet Admiral Montojo's squadron. At 5am, the light was sufficient to reveal that the Spanish warships were anchored to the south of the bay in a curve on the seaward side of the Cavite naval base promontory. Five minutes later, Dewey raised the flag signal to "prepare for general action" and steered the American squadron south toward the Spanish ships. The *McCulloch* and the two unarmed supply vessels were detached away from the coming battle.

Admiral Montojo had originally planned to fight Commodore Dewey in Subic Bay, away from the populated Manila Bay. Montojo had transferred guns from two of his ships to the islands governing the entrance to Subic Bay, and he ordered that the channels into the bay be mined. However, when he subsequently arrived in Subic Bay with his squadron, the guns had not been mounted in their battery and were therefore inoperable.

Admiral Montojo returned to Manila Bay and anchored under the guns of the Cavite and Sangley Point batteries. There were two advantages to this defensive position. It was away from the city of Manila and therefore saved the city and its civilian population from bombardment. Also, the waters off Cavite were shallow, and if his ships were sunk, their superstructure would remain above water, giving his crews a better opportunity to be rescued. Admiral Montojo realized that his ships, which were unarmored and relatively undergunned, stood little chance of defeating Dewey's squadron. To improve their survivability, Montojo had a number of steel lighters filled with sand and moored alongside his ships. In addition, top hamper was taken down from the masts and ships' boats taken ashore to avoid the risk of flying splinters, falling yards, and fire.

At 4am, Admiral Montojo signaled his squadron to prepare for action, and at 5:15am, the Spanish ships and the guns at Cavite opened fire on the approaching American squadron. On the open conning platform, Dewey waited until the range to the Spanish ships was down to 5,500 yards before taking action. Captain Charles Gridley of the *Olympia* was ordered to his action station in *Olympia*'s armored conning tower. At 5:40am, Dewey spoke into the voicepipe connecting the bridge to the conning tower, saying, "You may fire when you are ready, Gridley," and the right-hand 8-in. gun of *Olympia*'s forward turret opened fire.

Olympia off Mare Island in her original white Asiatic color scheme. The conning platform, seemingly suspended above the conning tower, is clearly visible. This platform was Dewey's location during the battle of Manila Bay.

The American ships passed from east to west along Montojo's moored ships, firing with their port batteries at 8 knots. At the end of the run of two miles, Dewey reversed the course of his squadron in succession and opened fire with his starboard batteries. During the second pass along the Spanish ships, Dewey closed the range to between 2,000 and 3,000 yards. Dewey led five passes along the Spanish ships, using alternate port and starboard batteries. During the fifth pass, amid the noise of the battle, with Dewey standing on the open bridge slightly aft of the forward gun turret, there was a miscommunication that led Dewey to understand that *Olympia*'s 5-in. guns had 15 rounds of ammunition left per gun. Dewey therefore led his squadron away from the battle at 7:35am to halt in mid-bay, at which time he called his captains to a conference and allowed the crews to have breakfast after two hours of battle. The miscommunication was corrected to the effect that the 5-in. guns had only *fired* 15 rounds each. Despite *Olympia* being hit six times and *Baltimore* five times, no American sailor had been killed. The Spanish ships had been badly damaged during this initial stage of the battle. The *Cristina* had attempted to charge the American line but had suffered a deluge of shells so that she had to be scuttled. Montojo moved his flag to *Isla de Cuba*.

Dewey returned to the battle at 11:16am, but only the *Ulloa* and the battery at Sangley Point were able to return fire. The *Ulloa* was promptly sunk, and the battery was silenced by *Baltimore*. Dewey ordered the *Petrel*, which had a shallow draft, to enter Cavite harbor and destroy the damaged ships, which she did by setting fire to *Isla de Cuba*, *Isla de Luzon*, *Don Juan de Austria*, *Marques del Duero*, and two other gunboats that had not been part of the Spanish line. The *Petrel* also took the surrender of the Spanish fort at Cavite, thereby securing the naval arsenal as a base for the US squadron. By 12:30pm, fighting had ceased. Commodore Dewey had achieved an overwhelming victory, and the *Olympia* had steered the United States to becoming a global naval power. Commodore Dewey was promoted to admiral to mark his success.

Dewey's squadron achieved 142 hits on the moored Spanish ships for an expenditure of 5,859 shells fired, representing a total hit rate of 2.42 percent. This was a sound performance, given the quality of the gun equipment of that time, the absence of a disciplined fire-control system, and the movements of Dewey's ships.

Another feature of the battle was the fact that Lieutenant Bradley Fiske, tied to a platform 45 feet up the foremast of the *Petrel*, was using his fire-control invention, the Stadimeter, to measure the range to the enemy. Fiske was to invent many fire-control instruments and become the foremost US naval authority on the concept and technical development of fire control. Unfortunately, a number of Fiske's inventions were perfected by other navies, and the US Navy had to buy them from foreign manufacturers.

 OFF SANGLEY POINT

The painting shows *Olympia* at 7:35am on May 1, 1898, at the end of her fifth pass along the Spanish line, off Sangley Point. At the end of each pass to the west, *Olympia* was adjacent to the two 5.9-in. Spanish guns in the Sangley Point battery at a range of only 1,500 yards. Fortunately for Dewey and his squadron, the Sangley Point battery had its guns sighted at 2,000 yards, thinking that no ship would come closer than that range. Consequently, the shells fired by these two guns flew over Dewey's ships.

E

The superstructure of the Spanish ship *Castilla* remained visible after she sank off Cavite. In the background, from left to right, are the US ships *Olympia*, *Baltimore*, and *Raleigh*.

USS *Charleston*, convoying US Army transports to Manila, took the surrender of the Spanish Pacific island of Guam, which was not even aware that a state of war existed between Spain and the United States.

The battle of Santiago

Sampson's battle squadron comprised his flagship, the *New York*, an armored cruiser with six 8-in. guns; the battleships *Iowa*, with four 12-in. guns, and the *Indiana* and *Oregon*, each with four 13-in. guns; and the armed yacht *Gloucester* with four 6pdrs. Sampson's command also included the Flying Squadron under the command of Commodore Winfield Schley. This comprised Schley's flagship, the armored cruiser *Brooklyn* with eight 8-in. guns, the battleship *Texas* with two 12-in. guns, the battleship *Massachusetts* with four 13-in. guns, and the armed yacht *Vixen* with four 6pdrs. Schley's Flying Squadron was initially based at Hampton Roads, Virginia, guarding the cities of the Eastern Seaboard from possible Spanish naval raids.

The US cruisers *Newark*, *San Francisco*, *Cincinnati*, *Minneapolis*, *Columbia*, *New Orleans*, *Montgomery*, and *Detroit* were employed blockading the Spanish Cuban ports and scouting for the Spanish squadron.

On April 29, Spain sent a squadron of armored cruisers across the Atlantic under the command of Admiral Pascual Cevera to counter the blockade. Cevera's squadron comprised four armored cruisers: his flagship, *Infanta Maria Teresa*, and *Almirante Oquendo*, *Viscaya*, and *Cristobal Colon*. The first three armored cruisers each carried a main armament of two 11-in. guns. *Cristobal Colon* was a new armored cruiser, but her main armament of two 10-in. guns had not been fitted. Therefore she only had her secondary armament of ten 6-in. guns. In addition, there were three torpedo boat destroyers, each mounting two 14pdrs and two 14-in. torpedo tubes.

Sampson expected Cevera to sail to San Juan on the island of Puerto Rico for coal. On May 12, Sampson bombarded San Juan to deny the facilities of this port to Cevera. Sampson did not know the location of Cevera's squadron until May 15, when he was advised that it had anchored in Martinique and then had sailed for Curacao. Sampson was concerned that Cevera would intercept the battleship *Oregon* that had to sail from San Francisco around Cape Horn and northward up the South American coast and across the Caribbean to join his command.

Sampson concentrated his command, including the Flying Squadron, at Key West on May 18. Following a conference with Schley, the Flying Squadron was ordered to blockade Cienfuegos, a port on Cuba's southern coast that was connected to Havana by rail. If Cevera had not reached Cienfuegos, Schley was to proceed to Santiago, another port, on the western end of Cuba's southern coast. Schley left for Cienfuegos on May 19, the day

Cevera entered Santiago harbor. Cevera's arrival was reported by a Cuban intelligence agent to Washington, D.C., and, in turn, relayed to Sampson. Schley was advised on May 23 and departed Cienfuegos the next day, after ensuring Cevera and his squadron were not in the port. Schley did not commence the blockade of Santiago until late on May 29. The slow speed of his auxiliary ships and bad weather that prevented coaling at sea, coupled with low onboard coal supplies, resulted in Schley passing Santiago and heading back to Key West for coal. However, on receipt of direct orders from Secretary Long, Schley returned to Santiago. A short duel with *Cristobal Colon* at the mouth of the harbor on May 30 produced no hits, and the *Colon* withdrew into the harbor behind its powerful fortifications. Sampson and his battleships arrived to join Schley on June 1.

Schley's problems with lack of coal forced Sampson to look for a nearby safe anchorage for coaling. USS *Marblehead* reconnoitered Guantanamo Bay and landed a party of US Marines to secure a beachhead on June 6. A Marine battalion landed on June 10 and established a camp to protect the ships that would use the anchorage. Guantanamo Bay provided the safe anchorage necessary for colliers to load Sampson's blockading ships with adequate supplies of coal. Additionally, the repair ship *Vulcan* undertook major repairs and provided technical supplies to the blockading ships. Both these factors gave Sampson strategic mobility for the forthcoming action. Sampson began the action with an attempt to block the narrow channel into Santiago harbor by sinking the collier *Merrimac* across the channel, but this attempt failed.

Faced with a blockading force of five battleships and two armored cruisers, Cevera remained in Santiago. Similarly, faced with the harbor's narrow and mined entrance and four coastal batteries, Sampson remained on blockade and relied on the US Army to land near Santiago, capture the city, and either force Cevera to leave or sink his ships at anchor. This was accomplished with Theodore Roosevelt's Rough Riders capturing San Juan Hill on July 1, and the US Army V Corps, under the command of General William Shafter, laying siege to Santiago by July 4. (Roosevelt had resigned his position at the Navy Department and had joined the Army for service in Cuba.)

Cevera was ordered to break through the blockade and sail for Cienfuegos or Havana, where the US naval blockading forces were relatively light. Cevera sailed on the morning of Sunday, July 3. His sortie caught the US blockading ships off guard. Sampson, on board his flagship *New York*, had sailed eastward away from Santiago to attend a conference with General Shafter, and the *Massachusetts* and several other smaller ships had sailed to Guantanamo Bay to coal. As a consequence, there were only eight ships on blockade, riding in a semicircle around the entrance to the harbor. The crews were enjoying Sunday service, and the ships were not stationed for action, a number with engines decoupled and boilers unfired.

Cristobal Colon and *Viscaya*, April 1898, before the battle of Santiago. Underarmed and without a secure supply of coal to provide strategic options, Admiral Cevera could only sail to defeat at Santiago.

The Washington Navy Yard was the manufacturer of all guns for the Navy. This 8-in. gun, situated midships on board the USS *New York*, shows a more sophisticated central mounting that enabled both fore and aft fire.

Recognizing the desperate plight of his squadron, Cevera ordered his flagship, *Infanta Maria Teresa*, to ram the *Brooklyn* after exiting Santiago harbor. His remaining ships might then have had sufficient speed to outrun the US battleships. *Brooklyn* avoided the ramming by circling away from *Teresa* and nearly collided with *Texas*. *Brooklyn* had the speed to catch up with the Spanish ships but only had two engines in use and could not afford to stop to recouple her two other engines. *Oregon* had kept all her boilers on line and was able to keep up with the *Brooklyn*. Together they poured a steady fire in the direction of the fleeing Spanish. Volumes of fire were high, and hits on the Spanish ships slowed them, bringing final gun ranges down to less than 1,000 yards. Within two hours, Cevera's squadron had been destroyed, with all four cruisers and one destroyer being run ashore to avoid sinking. Only one US sailor was killed during the battle, with the Spanish losing 323 killed.

The American fleet fired 9,433 shells at the Spanish ships and achieved 122 hits for a hit ratio of 1.29 percent. Unlike Manila Bay, where the hit ratio was 2.42 percent against moored targets, at Santiago the Spanish ships were sailing at high speed and maneuvering to avoid being hit. Initial gun ranges exceeded 4,000 yards, which was beyond the accuracy of range finders and the ranges at which gun crews had trained. Hits on the Spanish ships were only achieved when the ships were on parallel courses. However, the 122 hits were sufficient to destroy the Spanish vessels.

Under the terms of the Treaty of Paris, which ended the war between Spain and the United States on December 10, 1898, America gained possession of the Philippines, Puerto Rico, and Guam. Cuba gained its independence in 1902 and ceded Guantanamo Bay to the United States. American naval bases on Puerto Rico and Guantanamo Bay controlled the entrance and exit to the

USS *Maryland* under construction, just prior to launching at Newport News on September 12, 1903. The classic armored cruiser ram bow is clearly visible.

This is a view of the top of *Olympia*'s engine cylinders, which protrude through the protective deck. The top gray circle is the high pressure cylinder, with two valve heads adjacent. Armored glacis were placed across the opening during battle to give some protection, while still allowing ventilation. (Author's collection)

Caribbean and the future Panama Canal. Separately, Hawaii was finally annexed, giving America a string of naval stations across the Pacific.

The USS *Oregon* earned the nickname "McKinley's Bulldog" for her voyage around South America and the tenacious manner in which she kept up with the fleeing Spanish cruisers. The voyage of the *Oregon* increased the impetus for the United States to seek a canal across the isthmus of Central America. To that end, America helped Panama become an independent, sovereign nation, ceding from Colombia. The Hay-Bunau-Varilla Treaty of 1903 with Panama gave America control over the Canal Zone. America acquired the diggings, machinery, and infrastructure from the earlier failed French attempt to dig a canal. US Army engineers redesigned it, and the Panama Canal was completed in 1914.

Naval diplomacy

The US government exerted naval diplomacy through its growing fleet of cruisers. Battleships, as they were commissioned, were retained on the East Coast to protect the approaches to the main centers of population and economic activity. Compared to cruisers, battleships had limited range and were expensive to operate. US cruisers exerted diplomacy through their presence and that of landing parties of sailors and Marines from the Pacific to the Mediterranean. The more interesting examples of naval diplomacy were:

1893: The USS *Boston* landed a party of 162 sailors and Marines in Honolulu, Hawaii, in support of a revolution against Queen Lili'uokalani. This resulted in a Republic of Hawaii being established by the Committee of Public Safety, comprising leading American businessmen. Hawaii was formally annexed by the United States in 1898, following the Spanish-American War.

1900: Sailors and Marines from the USS *Newark* participated in the defense of a US legation in the siege of Peking (now Beijing) during the Boxer Rebellion in China. Sailors and Marines from the USS *Brooklyn* and *New Orleans* joined the international relief force that raised the siege.

One of *Olympia*'s cylinder pistons, connected via the crankshaft to the propeller shaft. Note the array of tools held in the bulkhead. (Author's collection)

1902: President Roosevelt exercised the oft-quoted maxim of "Walk softly, but carry a big stick" by appointing Admiral Dewey in November to command the Atlantic Fleet for its maneuvers in the Caribbean. These maneuvers coincided with Britain and Germany breaking diplomatic relations with Venezuela due to unpaid debts incurred by the Venezuelan government and their establishment of a naval blockade, comprising two cruisers and four gunboats/sloops from both navies.

Roosevelt was concerned that Germany would use the crisis to take possession of Venezuelan territory to establish a naval base for its growing navy, an action that would have been in conflict with the Monroe Doctrine. Roosevelt expanded the North Atlantic Squadron into the Atlantic Fleet, consisting of the Battleship Squadron, the Caribbean Squadron, and the Coast Squadron. Faced with the ships of the Atlantic Fleet and Roosevelt's confidential message that he would go to war, the Kaiser agreed to accept American arbitration. The blockade was lifted and the crisis passed. Roosevelt had followed Mahan's principle of concentrating naval force to ensure command of the sea.

1904: The USS *Brooklyn*, *Atlanta*, *Olympia*, *Baltimore*, and *Cleveland* anchored in Tangier harbor in late May to secure the release of American citizen Ion Pedicaris who had been kidnapped and held hostage by a bandit chief named Mohammed Raisuli. Raisuli was in conflict with the Sultan of Morocco. Pedicaris was released following a cable from President Roosevelt to the Sultan containing the words, "We want Pedicaris alive or Raisuli dead."

POINTING THE GUNS

Although the battles of Manila Bay and Santiago had been overwhelming successes, the low percentage of hits to shots fired concerned the US Navy. A detailed study by ONI, supported by reports from Lieutenant Fiske, identified the primary reasons for the poor gunnery results as a lack of range finders, a lack of telescopic sights on guns, a lack of gunnery practice, individual gun captains' firing decision process, and inadequate gun-training and elevating machinery to enable guns to be kept on target.

Lieutenants Fiske and William Sims drove the changes to improve gunnery in the US Navy. A critical dynamic in this process was the relationship Lieutenant Sims established with Captain Percy Scott of the Royal Navy during a meeting in Hong Kong in early March 1901. Captain Scott had produced a concept for gunnery that included gun equipment, specialized training equipment, criteria for selection of gunners, and competitive firing practice. Scott's concept had significantly improved gunnery results for the Royal Navy. Captain Scott shared the details of his system with Lieutenant Sims and continued to update him in the years that followed as the system developed to meet additional challenges to gun accuracy. This enabled Lieutenant Sims to establish himself at the forefront of changing the US Navy gunnery system to follow Captain Scott's concept and systems. Gun-training and elevating equipment was also modified across the fleet, giving gunners improved control to keep their guns on target.

Although gunnery results improved, increased gun ranges and ship speed meant that the objective of improved hitting itself became a moving target. Increased ranges meant that shells fired were affected by additional ballistic dynamics. Additionally, moving targets increased deflection measurements, further complicated by the movements of the firing ship. Both of these factors also increased gunnery control problems, necessitating the introduction of centralized fire control and new equipment. During this period, and notwithstanding Lieutenant Fiske's inventions, the US Navy found itself totally dependent upon British manufacturers for range finders and fire-control equipment. It was not until Elmer Sperry invented the gyroscope and perfected his "battle tracer" in 1918, together with Hannibal Ford's Rangekeeper (which incorporated Arthur Pollen's concepts for effective fire control and an identical copy of Pollen's integrator) that the US Navy had an effective fire-control system available from US manufacturers.

The men behind the guns

The men behind the guns of US warships in the 1880s were predominantly foreigners most of whom had been recruited in Northern Europe. Gunner's Mate Adolph Nilsson on board *Olympia*, thought to have fired the first shot in the battle of Manila Bay, joined the US Navy in Copenhagen in August 1885, at the age of 21. After serving 14 years with the Navy, he was honorably discharged in 1899, in New York, to become an American citizen. By 1899, after a series of reforms and improvements to a sailor's life, 75 percent of US sailors were US citizens. Additionally, during the period from 1880–91, the martial music of John Philip Sousa and the Marine Corps Band played a significant part in the promotion of the new navy to the US public and the recruitment of young American men.

The men behind the men behind the guns had been through a thorough educational process, beginning at the Naval Academy and on through to the NWC and postgraduate courses in engineering and naval architecture. Ongoing reforms increased the number of young officers needed for the new ships steadily being commissioned. Theodore Roosevelt vigorously proposed the amalgamation of the Engineering Corps with line officers, which was implemented in 1899. This reform created a more homogeneous officer corps, with officers trained in engineering and deck duties, and still able to specialize in technical areas.

A Driggs-Schroeder 6pdr quick-firing gun, with the breech open. These guns were used to deter or sink torpedo boats. (Author's collection)

USS *OLYMPIA*

The design of *Olympia* was an entirely domestic concept from the Corps of Naval Constructors and drew upon the experiences gained from earlier domestic and foreign-designed cruisers. Her unique and original design achieved a solid balance between hull shape, engine power, protection, and armament, leading to her long and successful career.

A large-scale wooden model of the hull was built from *Olympia*'s design plans. This model provided the basis for full-sized wooden templates to be made for hull plates and frames. Next, steel angle bars for hull frames were heated in a furnace

This is the duty engineer's station in the engine room, with the brass telegraph repeater. To the right are gauges measuring steam pressure at the cylinders. The brass and glass annunciator indicates which department is calling on the voice tube. (Author's collection)

and then placed on "bending slabs," where shipbuilders using sledge-hammers and bars forced the glowing steel around the steel pins that followed the template to produce the correct curvature. After this, steel plates were cast, usually 20 feet long, which were then run through giant steel rollers to form them to the required hull shape. Finally, punching machines pierced riveting holes in the plates and frames.

On the shipbuilding slipway, shipwrights laid the keel plates and attached the frames at specified locations, followed by stiffeners, the inner bottom deck, and the rest of the decks and bulkheads. Teams of riveters using sledgehammers pounded thousands of red-hot rivets into place to hold the ship together. Engines and boilers were lifted into place, and the ship was launched and placed alongside a fitting-out pier where the superstructure, armaments, and internal equipment were fitted.

Olympia was constructed from mild open-hearth 1010 low carbon steel, with the outer keel plate being ⁹⁄₁₆in. thick. The outside plating was ½in. thick, attached to 91 frames that were spaced four feet apart over the 160-foot length of the double bottom. Within the space of the hull were four longitudinal bulkheads, with the two innermost being watertight.

The protective deck was 2in. thick but increased to 4¾in. on the sloping sides covering the machinery spaces. The armor was reduced to 3in. forward and aft of the machinery space. As the cylinder heads of the engine protruded above the protective deck, they were shielded by a series of glacis plates 4in. thick, inclined at 30 degrees.

 USS *OLYMPIA* TODAY

This photograph shows the USS *Olympia* in July 2007, moored at Penn's Landing, with ongoing restoration in process. Both the teak wheelhouse and ship's boats have been removed for restoration work. The photograph shows the closed bow torpedo tube. *Olympia* is riding approximately four feet higher in the bow as a result of the absence of coal, ammunition, torpedo tubes, and her complement of crew. The clean, sweeping lines of the ship and the uncluttered superstructure are clearly evident. The ship is painted in the colors of her triumphal entry to New York in 1899.

Olympia's protection was enhanced by 153 watertight compartments. Cofferdams extending alongside the machinery spaces at water level were filled with cellulose material, corn husks, and coconut fiber. In the event of the hull being penetrated, the cellulose material would expand to absorb the water and fill the hole. Coal bunkers also provided protection for the machinery spaces.

Olympia was powered by two vertical three-cylinder, triple-expansion reciprocating engines, separated by a midships watertight bulkhead. The engines were rated at 13,500hp utilizing 160 pounds of pressure at 128 revolutions per minute. The steam pressure was delivered from six boilers, four of which were double-ended, measuring 15ft 3in. in diameter and 21ft 3in. long. The two single-ended boilers produced sufficient pressure to generate power and steam when not under way. During her trials, *Olympia*'s engines produced in excess of 17,300hp and a speed of 21.7 knots. With full coal bunkers, *Olympia* could steam 6,000 miles.

Olympia was the only protected cruiser to be fitted with cylindrical gun turrets as used on the Civil War monitors. The two turrets on the centerline, one forward, the other aft, each mounted two 8-in. guns. Ten 5-in. quick-firing guns were mounted in casemates, five per beam. These newly designed guns could fire in excess of three shells per minute. *Olympia* also carried six torpedoes in above-water tubes, one tube in the bow, one in the stern, and two on each beam.

Olympia was designed as a flagship for the Asiatic Squadron and carried admiral's quarters. In addition, she was fitted with the first onboard refrigeration plant as part of her auxiliary equipment, to improve habitability in the tropics.

Following her commissioning on February 5, 1895, and after several months breaking in her new crew, the USS *Olympia* sailed from San Francisco on August 25, 1895, for her new station in Asia. Over the next three years she showed the flag in Japan, China, Korea, Russia, and Hong Kong. Commodore Dewey raised his flag on board the *Olympia* on January 3, 1898, at Nagasaki. During April she returned to Hong Kong and prepared for war with Spain. On May 1, she led the Asiatic Squadron to victory at Manila Bay against the Spanish squadron. *Olympia* stayed on station in Manila Bay for over one year as the United States established control over the Philippines, leaving for Hong Kong in May 1899. *Olympia* returned to the United States via the Suez Canal and Gibraltar, anchoring off New York on September 26, 1899. Dewey was formally welcomed to New York by the now-governor, Theodore Roosevelt, who, as Under Secretary of the Navy, had been responsible for appointing Commodore Dewey to command the Asiatic Squadron in 1898.

In October 1899, she then arrived in the Boston Navy Yard for an overdue refit, having completed four years of continuous sea duty. The refit took several years and included new ammunition hoists for her main turrets as well as electric motors to turn them, improved coal-loading equipment, removal of the six torpedo tubes, an enlarged pilot house and aft bridge deck, and a lifting boom on the main mast. Equally important, the ship was rid of the tropical insects that lived in her wooden fittings and the cellulose material in her cofferdams that had rotted. Upon completion, *Olympia* joined the North Atlantic Station where she sailed the east coast of the United States and throughout the Caribbean.

In June 1902, *Olympia* was fitted with a Marconi wireless telegraph. This was a low-frequency sparkgap 1kW transmitter and required fidded topmasts to be added to both fore and main masts to carry the antennae. On October 4, 1902, *Olympia* became flagship of the Caribbean Squadron as part of the new Atlantic Fleet that was under the command of Admiral Dewey.

In 1904, *Olympia* cruised around Europe and Great Britain, returning to the Caribbean in early 1905, where she became flagship of the Third Squadron of the North Atlantic Fleet. In April 1906, she was taken out of commission at Norfolk Navy Yard and was given an internal refit of her berthing arrangements. However, naval technology had rapidly advanced since *Olympia*'s original design, and the Navy relegated her to a midshipman's training ship at Annapolis. She remained in this role until August 1909, when she was further relegated to reserve status without participating in the annual training cruises. In 1912, *Olympia* was transferred to the Charleston Navy Yard as a barrack ship for a destroyer division. From January–June 1915, she was in commission safeguarding American interests in Mexico during one of the Mexican revolutions, and at the end of this period she returned to Charleston and reserve status. In 1916, *Olympia* underwent a major refit at Charleston, with her two 8-in. gun turrets being removed and replaced by single 4-in. guns. In addition, the 5-in. rapid-fire guns were removed and were also replaced with 4-in. guns.

The entry of America into World War I in April 1917 saw the *Olympia* recommissioned as the flagship of the Atlantic Patrol Force on antisubmarine duty. On entering Long Island Sound on June 25, 1917, she ran aground and ripped open her hull. Repairs and replacement of her 4-in. guns with 5-in. guns at the Brooklyn Navy Yard took eight months. From February to April 1918, *Olympia* undertook convoy duty in the Atlantic. She was dry-docked in Charleston in mid-April and had her internal berthing remodeled for improved accommodation for her next mission. On April 28, *Olympia* sailed for Scapa Flow, the anchorage of the Royal Navy Grand Fleet and the US Battle Squadron, located in the Orkney Islands. She took on the British military representative to Russia and a French civil mission and then sailed for Murmansk. The primary objective was to reinforce an Allied contingent

A 5-in./.51-cal. secondary armament gun on the gun deck. The interrupted screw breech mechanism is clearly visible along with the mushroom cap on the inside of the breech plug. This cap creates the final seal for the breech when the gun is fired. (Author's collection)

defending Murmansk and the railhead carrying supplies to Russia from a German attack through Finland. 110 crew members were launched to police Murmansk. Subsequently, *Olympia* sent a force of 50 crew members to Archangel as part of an Allied force of 1,300 troops. These crew members were in action against the Red Army. *Olympia* left Murmansk in November 1918, and arrived in Portsmouth, England, at the end of the month for dry-docking. Sailing for Venice on December 26, she took up station along the Dalmatian coast, policing the dispute between Austria and Italy following the armistice. In August 1919, *Olympia* sailed for Constantinople, now Istanbul, and then on to the Black Sea, returning to the Dalmatian coast in mid-September, where her landing party prevented hostilities from occurring between Italian and Yugoslav forces. She returned to Charleston in November 1919.

In April 1920, *Olympia* became flagship of the US naval forces in the Adriatic and continued patrolling the Dalmatian coast, with side visits to Italian ports, before sailing for the Philadelphia Navy Yard to become flagship for the Train of the Atlantic Fleet in June. In this role, *Olympia* was part of the observation fleet to the aerial bombardment and sinking of surrendered German warships by Billy Mitchell's Army bombers.

Following dry-docking at Norfolk Navy Yard in September 1921, *Olympia* sailed for Europe for a unique honor that reflected her historic standing both in the US Navy and with the American populace. At 3pm on October 15, 1921, the body of an unknown American soldier was carried on board *Olympia*, docked at Le Havre, France, marked by solemn ceremonies with French and American dignitaries in attendance. She returned the Unknown Soldier to US soil, arriving at the Washington Navy Yard on November 9, and was met by a cortege that accompanied the body to its lying in state on Capitol Hill, prior to its internment in the Tomb of the Unknown Soldier at Arlington.

Olympia spent the final year of her commission as a training ship for Annapolis midshipmen on their cruise through the Caribbean and North Atlantic. On December 9, 1922, she was decommissioned and laid up at the Philadelphia Navy Yard. The USS *Olympia* was declared a National Historic Monument in 1976, with its engines declared a National Historic Engineering Landmark in 1987.

Today, the USS *Olympia*, in her early 1902 configuration and peacetime colors of white hull and cream superstructure, is moored at Penn's Landing on the Delaware River in Philadelphia, Pennsylvania. The USS *Olympia* is part of the Independence Seaport Museum, a short walk from Philadelphia's Independence Hall and the Liberty Bell. The museum assumed full responsibility for the ship in January 1996, to ensure that the sole survivor of the new navy, and the ship that steered the United States to global power, remains open to the public. The restoration of USS *Olympia* remains an ongoing project.

Olympia's final berthing at Penn's Landing, Philadelphia, recognizes the unique role this city and the Delaware River basin played in the development of the new steel navy and the Asiatic Squadron in particular. The shipbuilding and industrial skills and expertise developed in and around Philadelphia, coupled with the steel and armor produced in the state of Pennsylvania by Bethlehem, Carnegie, and Midvale, created a substantial naval arsenal and helped lay the foundation for the modern US Navy.

CONCLUSION

In the space of 15 years, 1883–98, the US Navy climbed from obsolescent obscurity to become a global naval power at Manila Bay. The authorization of 39 cruisers from 1883 to 1904 was the foundation stone of this power.

The early cruisers were of questionable design and capability. However, with the USS *Olympia* and subsequent cruisers, the US Navy obtained world-class warships. The major weakness for all the cruisers was the lack of adequate optical and ordnance equipment, together with a disciplined gunnery-control system. A naval fleet engagement during this period with the Royal Navy, German, or Japanese navies would have been a very high-risk venture.

The critical feature of the US cruiser program was the impetus it gave to US industry to develop sophisticated steel and shipbuilding industries during

Looking forward through the engine room with the propeller shaft running underneath the stair treads. The wooden barrel in the top right is the engine condenser, which cools the steam back to water before returning it to the boilers. (Author's collection)

a period of rapid naval technological change. The design and construction of these 39 cruisers provided the experience and expertise to build larger and more complex battleships. Additionally, the development of these industries generated major economic developments in non-military areas of the US economy with increasing technological inventiveness. The peacetime military build-up of the Navy provided the shipbuilding infrastructure for subsequent rapid wartime shipbuilding in World War I and World War II.

The lessons of the Spanish-American War provided the clarity for the development of a naval strategy based upon a two-ocean-capable navy, built around capital ships able to engage in fleet actions.

Although the flag initially followed the trader and missionary, particularly in the Pacific and China, the rapidly growing US Navy, in turn, gave US diplomacy an increasing capability and gravitas to support a developing robust US foreign policy. This was clearly demonstrated in November–December 1902, during the Venezuelan crisis with Germany and Britain and the subsequent voyage of the Great White Fleet.

The reform process for naval personnel took many years to become effective. The enlistment of young Americans, the establishment of ONI and NWC, the residual war experience of Civil War officers, and the overwhelming naval victories at Manila Bay and Santiago all laid the foundation for the emergence of highly professional and well-trained sailors capable of successfully wielding the immense power of the US Navy.

SELECT BIBLIOGRAPHY

BOOKS
Alden, John D., Commander, US Navy (Retired), *The American Steel Navy*, Naval Institute Press, Annapolis, Maryland (1972)

Cooling, Benjamin Franklin, *Benjamin Franklin Tracy: Father of the Modern American Fighting Navy*, Archon Books, North Haven, Connecticut (1973)

_____ *Gray Steel and Blue Water Navy: The Formative Years of America's Military-Industrial Complex 1881–1917*, Archon Books, North Haven, Connecticut (1979)

A view across a boiler room, with the fire grates on the left. A coal bunker door is open, and coal is emerging from underneath the watertight door. (Author's collection)

_____ *USS Olympia: Herald of Empire*, Naval Institute Press, Annapolis, Maryland (2000)

Crawford, Michael, Mark Hayes, and Michael Sessions, *The Spanish-American War: Historical Overview and Selected Bibliography*, Naval Historical Center, Washington, D.C. (1998)

Dewey, Admiral of the Navy George, *Autobiography of George Dewey*, Naval Institute Press, Annapolis, Maryland (1987)

Fiske, Rear-Admiral Bradley A., *From Midshipman to Rear-Admiral*, T. Werner Laurie, Ltd. (1919)

Friedman, Norman, *U.S. Cruisers: An Illustrated Design History*, Naval Institute Press, Annapolis, Maryland (1984)

Hattendorf, John B., B. Mitchell Simpson III, and John R. Wadleigh, *Sailors and Scholars*, Naval War College Press, Newport, Rhode Island (1984)

Havern, Christopher B., *A Gunnery Revolution Manqué: William S. Sims and the adoption of Continuous-Aim in the United States Navy, 1898–1910*. Masters Thesis. University of Maryland

Hayes, Mark, *War Plans and Preparations and Their Impact on U.S. Naval Operations in the Spanish-American War*, Naval Historical Center, Washington, D.C. (1998)

Marolda, Edward, ed., *Theodore Roosevelt, the U.S. Navy, and the Spanish-American War*, New York, Palgrave (2001)

Musicant, Ivan, *U.S. Armored Cruisers: A Design and Operational History*, Naval Institute Press, Annapolis, Maryland (1985)

Roosevelt, Theodore, *The Naval War of 1812*, Cambridge, Massachusetts, Da Capo Press (1999)

Schulman, Mark Russell, *Navalism and the Emergence of American Sea Power: 1882–1893*, Annapolis, Maryland, Naval Institute Press (1995)

NEWSPAPERS
The Hong Kong Weekly Press, April 30, May 7, and May 14, 1898. Hong Kong Government Records Office

WEB SITES
http://www.history.navy.mil/index.html
http://www.spanamwar.com/index.htm
http://www.hnsa.org/index.ht

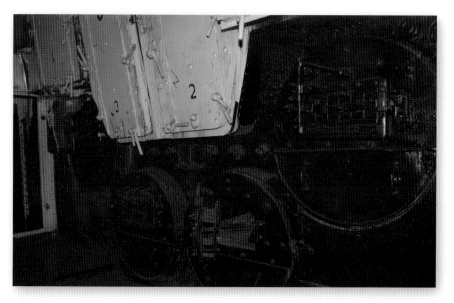

The four fire boxes in the boiler room. These boilers are double ended, with another crew on the other side. Twelve men would serve these fire boxes, with additional men in the coal bunkers moving coal to the bunker door. (Author's collection)

APPENDIX

US CRUISERS: DESIGN SPECIFICATIONS

	Atlanta/Boston	Chicago	Newark	Charleston
Waterline load length	270ft 3in.	325ft	310ft	312ft
Beam	42ft	48ft 2in.	49ft 2in.	46ft
Draft	17ft	19ft	18ft 9in.	19ft 7in.
Displacement	3,189 tons	4,500 tons	4,083 tons	4,040 tons
Armament	2 x 8-in./.30-cal. 6 x 6-in./.30-cal. 2 x 6pdr; 2 x 3pdr 2 x 1pdr; 2 x 47mm 2 x 37mm	4 x 8-in./.30-cal. 8 x 6-in./.30-cal. 2 x 5-in./.30-cal. 2 x 6pdr; 2 x 1pdr 4 x 47mm; 2 x 37mm 2 x Gatlings	12 x 6-in./.30-cal. 4 x 6pdr; 4 x 3pdr 2 x 1pdr; 2 x 37mm	2 x 8-in./.35-cal. 6 x 6-in./.30-cal. 4 x 6pdr; 2 x 3pdr 2 x 1pdr; 4 x 37mm 2 Gatlings
Torpedo tubes	none	none	Openings for 6 x 14-in., above-surface tubes	Openings for 4 x 14-in., above-surface tubes
Armor protection	Sloping and flat armor deck 1½ in.	Sloping and flat armor deck 1½in.	Sloping 3-in. and flat armor deck 2-in.	Sloping 3-in. and flat armor deck 2-in.
Machinery	Horizontal compound engine to single screw, with auxiliary brig sail rig of 10,400 sq. ft	Compound overhead beam engines to twin-screws, with auxiliary bark sail rig of 14,880 sq. ft	Horizontal triple-expansion engines to twin screw, with auxiliary bark sail rig of 11,932 sq. ft	Horizontal compound engines to twin screws
Performance	4,030hp = 15.60kts	5,084hp = 15.33kts	8,869hp=19kts	6,666hp=18.21kts
Complement	19 officers. 265 enlisted men	33 officers. 376 enlisted men	34 officers. 350 enlisted men	20 officers. 280 enlisted men

	Baltimore	Philadelphia	San Francisco	Olympia
Waterline load length	327ft 6in.	327ft 6in.	310ft	340ft
Beam	48ft 6in.	48ft 6in.	49ft 2in.	53ft ⅝in.
Draft	20ft 6in.	19ft 2½in.	18ft 9in.	21ft 6in.
Displacement	4,600 tons	4,324 tons	4,083 tons	5,870 tons
Armament	4 x 8-in./.35-cal. 6 x 6-in./.30-cal. 4 x 6pdr; 2 x 3pdr 2 x 1pdr; 4 x 37mm	12 x 6-in./.30-cal. 4 x 6pdr; 4 x 3pdr 2 x 1pdr; 3 x 37mm	12 x 6-in./.30-cal. 4 x 6pdr; 4 x 3pdr 2 x 1pdr; 3 x 37mm	4 x 8-in./.35-cal. 10 x 5-in./.40-cal. 14 x 6pdr; 6 x 1pdr 4 Gatlings
Torpedo tubes	Openings for 5 x 14-in., above-surface tubes	Openings for 4 x 14-in., above-surface tubes	Openings for 6 x 14-in., above-surface tubes	6 x 18-in. Whitehead above-surface tubes
Armor protection	Sloping 4-in. and flat armor deck 2½-in.	Sloping 4-in. and flat armor deck 2½-in.	Sloping 4-in. and flat armor deck 2½-in.	Sloping 4¾-in. and flat armor deck 2-in.
Machinery	Horizontal triple-expansion engines to twin screws.	Horizontal triple-expansion engines to twin screws, with auxiliary schooner rig	Horizontal triple-expansion engines to twin screws with auxiliary schooner rig	Vertical triple-expansion engines to twin screws with auxiliary schooner rig
Performance	10,064hp = 19.58kts	8,814hp = 19.68kts	9,913hp = 19.52kts	17,313hp = 21.69kts
Complement	36 officers. 350 enlisted men	34 officers. 350 enlisted men	34 officers. 350 enlisted men	33 officers. 395 enlisted men

	Cincinnati Class	Montgomery Class	New York	Columbia Class	Brooklyn
Waterline load length	300ft	257ft	380ft 6½in.	412ft	400ft 6in.
Beam	42ft	37ft	64ft 10in.	58ft 2¼-in.	64ft 8¼in.
Draft	18ft	14ft 7in.	23ft 3 ½in.	22ft 6 ½-in.	24ft
Displacement	3,213 tons	2,094 tons	8,200 tons	7,375 tons	9,215 tons
Armament	1 x 6-in./.40-cal. 10 x 5-in./.40-cal. 8 x 6pdr; 4 x 1pdr 2 Gatlings	2 x 6-in./.40-cal. 8 x 5-in./.40-cal. 6 x 6pdr; 2 x 1pdr 2 Gatlings	6 x 8-in./.35-cal. 12 x 4in./.40-cal. 8 x 6-pdr; 4 x 1pdr 4 Gatlings	1 x 8-in./.40-cal. 2 x 6-in./.40-cal. 8 x 4-in./.40-cal. 12 x 6pdr; 4 x 1pdr 4 Gatlings	8 x 8-in./.35-cal. 12 x 5in./.40-cal. 12 x 6pdr; 4 x 1pdr 4 Gatlings
Torpedo tubes	4 above-surface tubes	3 above-surface tubes	3 x 18-in. Whitehead above-surface tubes	4 x 14-in. Whitehead above-surface tubes	4 x 18-in. Whitehead above-surface tubes
Armor protection	Sloping 2½-in. and flat armor deck 1-in.	Sloping ⅞₆-in. and flat armor deck ⅝₆-in.	Sides 4-in. and turrets armor 5½-in.	Sloping 4-in. and flat armor deck 2½-in.	Sides 3-in. and turret armor 5½-in.
Machinery	Vertical triple-expansion engines to twin screws with auxiliary schooner rig	Vertical triple-expansion engines to twin screws with auxiliary schooner rig	Four vertical triple-expansion engines to twin screws	Three vertical triple-expansion engines to triple screws with auxiliary schooner rig	Four vertical triple-expansion engines to twin screws
Performance	10,000hp = 19kts	5,527hp = 19.05kts	17,401hp = 21kts	18,509hp = 22.8kts	18,769hp = 21.91kts
Complement	20 officers. 292 enlisted men	20 officers. 254 enlisted men	40 officers. 526 enlisted men	30 officers. 429 enlisted men	46 officers. 470 enlisted men

	New Orleans Class	Pennsylvania Class	Denver Class	St. Louis Class	Tennessee Class
Waterline load length	346ft	502ft	292ft	424ft	502ft
Beam	43ft 9in.	69ft 6½in.	44ft ½in.	66ft	72ft 10½in.
Draft	16ft 10⅓-in.	24ft 1in.	15ft 9in.	22ft 6in.	25ft
Displacement	3,437 tons	13,680 tons	3,191 tons	9,700 tons	14,500 tons
Armament	6 x 6-in./.50-cal. 4 x 4.7in./.50-cal. 10 x 6pdr; 4 x 1pdr 4 x .30-cal.	4 x 8-in./.40-cal. 14 x 6-in./.50-cal. 18 x 3-in.; 12 x 3pdr; 4 x 1pdr; 6 x .30-cal.	10 x 5-in./.50-cal. 8 x 6pdr; 2 x 1pdr; 4 x .30-cal.	14 x 6-in./.50-cal. 18 x 3-in.; 12 x 3pdr 8 x 1-pdr; 4 x .30-cal.	4 x 10-in./.40-cal. 16 x 6in./.50-cal. 22 x 3-in.; 12 x 3pdr 2 x 1pdr; 6 x .30-cal.
Torpedo tubes	3 x 18-in. Whitehead above-surface tubes	2 x 18-in. submerged tubes	none	none	4 x 21-in. submerged tubes
Armor protection	Sloping 3-in. and flat armor deck 1¼-in.	Side belt 6-in.; turrets 6½-in.	Sloping 2-in. and flat armor deck ½-in.	Sides 4-in.	Sides 5-in and turrets armor 9-in.
Machinery	Vertical inverted triple-expansion engine to twin screw	Vertical triple expansion engines to twin-screws	Vertical triple-expansion engine to twin screws with auxiliary schooner rig	Vertical triple-expansion engine to twin screws	Vertical triple-expansion engine to twin screws
Performance	7,500hp = 20kts	28,600hp = 22.44kts	6,135hp = 16.75kts	27,264hp = 22.13kts	26,963hp = 22.16kts
Complement	24 officers. 383 enlisted men	41 officers. 791 enlisted men	19 officers. 308 enlisted men	36 officers. 627 enlisted men	40 officers. 874 enlisted men

INDEX

Figures in **bold** refer to illustrations.